It's My Body

Legs and Feet

Lola Schaefer

www.raintreepublishers.co.uk
Visit our website to find out more information about **Raintree** books.

To order:
- ☎ Phone 44 (0) 1865 888112
- 🗎 Send a fax to 44 (0) 1865 314091
- 💻 Visit the Raintree Bookshop at **www.raintreepublishers.co.uk** to browse our catalogue and order online.

First published in Great Britain by Raintree, Halley Court, Jordan Hill, Oxford OX2 8EJ, part of Harcourt Education.
Raintree is a registered trademark of Harcourt Education Ltd.

Editorial: Jennifer Gillis and Diyan Leake
Design: Sue Emerson and Michelle Lisseter
Picture Research: Jennifer Gillis
Production: Lorraine Hicks

Originated by Dot Gradations
Printed and bound in China by South China Printing Company

ISBN 1 844 21650 0
07 06 05 04 03
10 9 8 7 6 5 4 3 2 1

British Library Cataloguing in Publication Data
Schaefer, Lola
Legs and feet
612.9'8
A full catalogue record for this book is available from the British Library.

Acknowledgements
The publishers would like to thank the following for permission to reproduce photographs: Corbis pp. 9 (Chris Carroll), 13 (Kari Weatherly), 16 (Charles O'Rear), 20 (George Shelley), 21 (Paul Barton), 23 (heel, George Shelley); Corbis Stock Market pp. 17 (Ted Horowitz), back cover (toes); Custom Medical Stock Photo pp. 10, 23 (bone, joint); Heinemann Library pp. 4 (Robert Lifson), 6 (Brian Warling), 8 (Robert Lifson), 14 (Robert Lifson), 15 (Brian Warling), 22 (Brian Warling), 23 (ankle, hip, knee, Brian Warling), 24 (Brian Warling), back cover (knee, Brian Warling); PhotoTake p. 18 (Collection CNRI); PictureQuest pp. 5 (Vic Thomasson/Rex Intstock/Stock Connection), 7 (Ginny Nichols/Stock Connection), 12 (Bob Daemmrich/Stock Boston Inc.), 19 (DigitalVision), 23 (muscles, Ginny Nichols/Stock Connection).

Cover photograph reproduced with permission of Corbis (Larry Williams).

Every effort has been made to contact copyright holders of any material reproduced in this book. Any omissions will be rectified in subsequent printings if notice is given to the publishers.

Some words are shown in bold, **like this.** You can find them in the glossary on page 23.

Contents

What are my legs and feet? 4

Where are my legs? 6

What do my legs look like? 8

What is inside my legs? 10

What can I do with my legs? 12

Where are my feet? 14

What are the parts of my feet?. 16

What is inside my feet? 18

What can I do with my feet? 20

Quiz. 22

Glossary 23

Index 24

Answers to quiz 24

What are my legs and feet?

Legs and feet are parts of your body.

Your body is made up of many parts.

Each part of your body does a job.

You use your legs and feet to stand, walk and play.

Where are my legs?

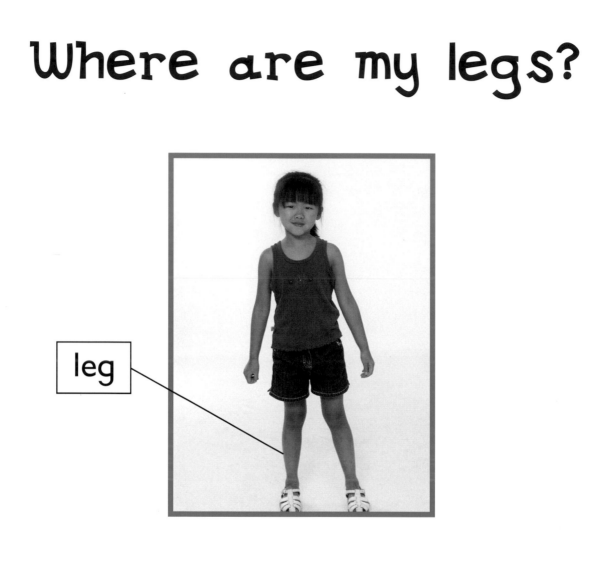

leg

Your legs are under your body.

They hold up your body.

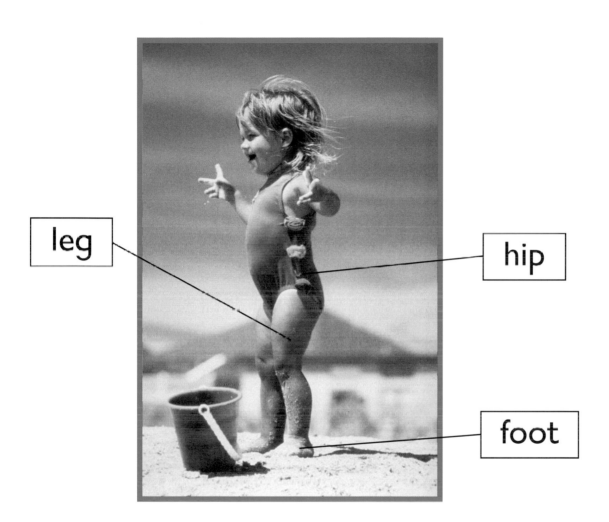

leg

hip

foot

Legs join your body at your **hips**.

Legs are between your hips
and feet.

What do my legs look like?

Legs are long **limbs** covered in skin.

You have two legs.

You can bend your legs.

You can stretch your legs
out straight.

What is inside my legs?

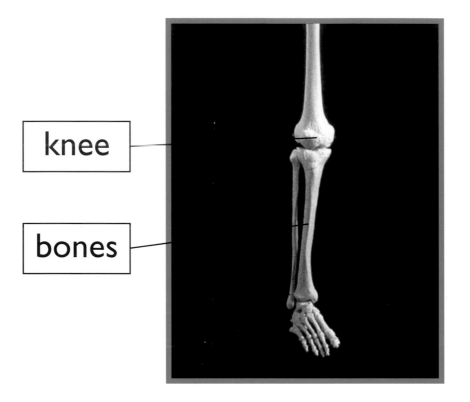

knee

bones

There are **bones** inside your legs.

Your leg bones meet at your **knee**.

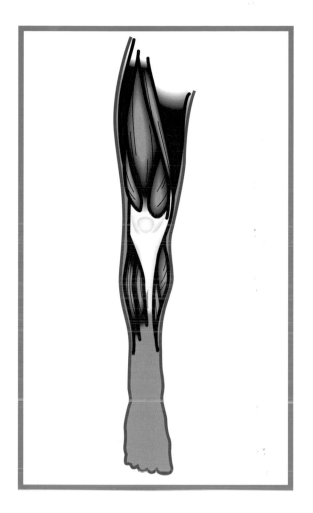

There are **muscles** inside your legs.

You use your muscles to make your **bones** move.

What can I do with my legs?

You can stand on your legs.

You use your legs when you dance.

You use your legs when you run
and jump.

You use them when you ride
a bike.

Where are my feet?

Feet are at the ends of your legs.

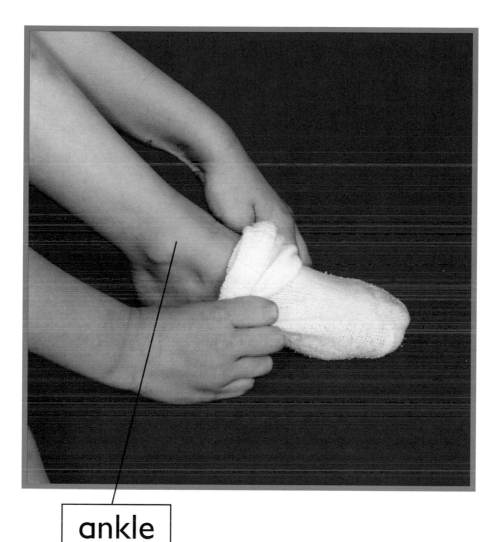

ankle

Ankles join your feet to your legs.

Ankles are **joints** that help your feet move.

What are the parts of my feet?

The bottom of each foot is the sole.

You can make **footprints** with your soles.

You have five toes at the front of each foot.

The back of each foot is the heel.

What is inside my feet?

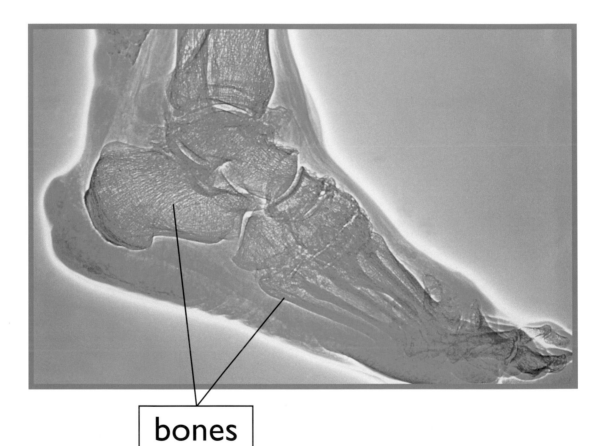

bones

There are **bones** inside your feet.

Some bones are big and some are small.

There are **muscles** inside your feet.

You use your muscles to move the bones in your feet.

What can I do with my feet?

Your feet help you stand.

You kick with your feet when you swim.

Your feet can grip what is beneath them.

You can kick a ball with your feet.

Quiz

Do you know what these are?

Look for the answers on page 24.

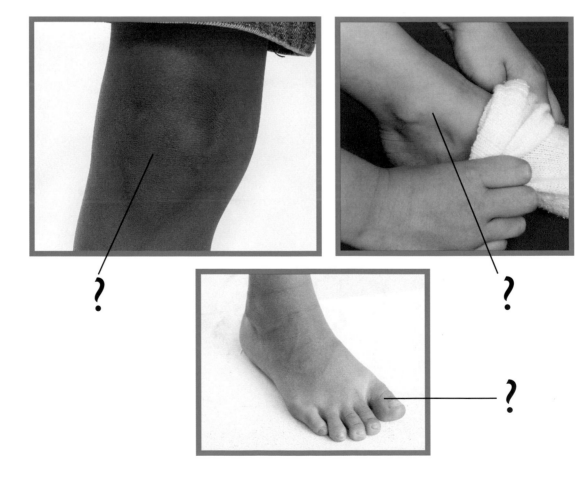

?

?

?

Glossary

ankle
the joint between your foot and your leg

bone
hard part inside your body

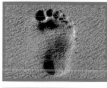

footprint
the mark made by your foot

hip
the joint between your leg and your body

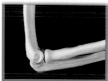

joint
a part of your body where bones come together so they can move

knee
the joint in your leg

limb
arm or leg

muscle
a part in your body that you use to move with

Index

ankles   15, 23

body   4, 5, 6, 7

bones   10, 11, 18, 19, 23

heels   17

hips   7, 23

joints   15, 23

knees   10, 23

muscles   11, 19, 23

skin   8

toes   17

Answers to quiz on page 22

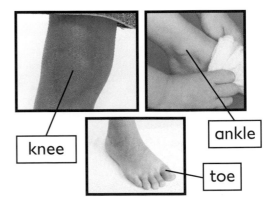

knee

ankle

toe

24

Titles in the It's My Body series include:

Hardback   1 844 21647 0

Hardback   1 844 21648 9

Hardback   1 844 21649 7

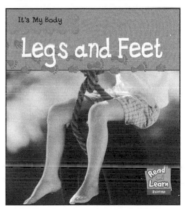

Hardback   1 844 21650 0

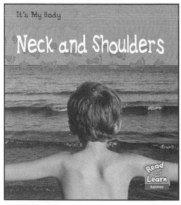

Hardback   1 844 21651 9

Find out about the other titles in this series on our website www.raintreepublishers.co.uk